DIGGING UP
the Past

Chaco Canyon

Essential Library

An Imprint of Abdo Publishing | www.abdopublishing.com

Chaco Canyon

BY CHRIS EBOCH

CONTENT CONSULTANT
JAKOB SEDIG
PHD CANDIDATE
UNIVERSITY OF COLORADO, BOULDER

www.abdopublishing.com

Published by Abdo Publishing, a division of ABDO, PO Box 398166, Minneapolis, Minnesota 55439. Copyright © 2015 by Abdo Consulting Group, Inc. International copyrights reserved in all countries. No part of this book may be reproduced in any form without written permission from the publisher. Essential Library™ is a trademark and logo of Abdo Publishing.

Printed in the United States of America, North Mankato, Minnesota
032014
092014

THIS BOOK CONTAINS
RECYCLED MATERIALS

Cover Photo: Josemaria Toscano/Shutterstock Images
Interior Photos: Josemaria Toscano/Shutterstock Images, 2; George H. H. Huey/Corbis, 6; W. Langdon Kihn/National Geographic Society/Corbis, 9; iStockphoto/Thinkstock, 11; Rainer Lesniewski/Shutterstock Images, 11 (inset); Marilyn Angel Wynn/Nativestock Pictures/Corbis, 13; Eric Draper/AP Images, 14; Bettmann/Corbis, 17, 45; Tim Pleasant/Shutterstock Images, 20; Alexey Kamenskiy/Shutterstock Images, 21; Macduff Everton/Corbis, 24; Charles Martin/National Geographic Image Collection/Glow Images, 28, 93; Roy H. Anderson/National Geographic/Getty Images, 33, 47; National Park Service, 38, 41, 58, 72, 82; NASA, 50; Dewitt Jones/Corbis, 53; Robert Mandel/Shutterstock Images, 57; The Daily Times/Marc F. Henning/AP Images, 62; O. C. Havens/National Geographic Society/Corbis, 64; Jeff Geissler/AP Images, 67; Dewitt Jones/Corbis/Glow Images, 70; Michael Runkel/SuperStock, 75; James Hager/Robert Harding World Imagery/Corbis, 76; Scott T. Smith/Corbis, 80; Danny Lehman/Corbis, 86; Fred Hirschmann/Science Faction/Corbis, 89; Michael Melford/National Geographic Society/Corbis, 97

Editor: Arnold Ringstad
Series Designer: Becky Daum

Library of Congress Control Number: 2014932245

Cataloging-in-Publication Data

Eboch, Chris.
 Chaco Canyon / Chris Eboch.
  p. cm. -- (Digging up the past)
Includes bibliographical references and index.
ISBN 978-1-62403-231-8
1. Chaco culture--New Mexico--Chaco Canyon--Antiquities-- Juvenile literature. 2. Cliff-dwellings--New Mexico--Chaco Canyon--Juvenile literature. 3. Chaco Canyon (N.M.)--Antiquities--Juvenile literature.   4. Chaco Culture National Historical Park (N.M.)--Juvenile literature. I. Title.
978.9/2--dc23
                                                              2014932245

CONTENTS

1

Secrets of the Past

When people think of the great civilizations of the past, they may picture Egyptian pyramids, Greek temples, or the Great Wall of China. But North America had its own powerful cultures centuries ago. Native Americans established one of the greatest cities of all time more than 1,000 years ago in what is now the southwestern United States. In a harsh landscape with little water and short growing seasons, a vast and complex city emerged.

Chaco Canyon is among the most important archaeological sites in North America.

THE RISE AND FALL OF THE ANCIENT ONES

Before the 800s CE, the only settlements around Chaco Canyon were small household groups. Between 850 and 925, people began constructing large buildings containing hundreds of rooms. An even greater period of construction occurred between 1020 and 1140. Then new construction slowed and neighboring communities took more power. Over time, Chaco's people migrated to new areas and eventually mixed with other cultures.

Its ruins reside in a remote corner of northwestern New Mexico, in Chaco Canyon.

The canyon itself is 15 miles (24 km) long and up to one mile (1.6 km) wide. A stream known as the Chaco Wash cut the shallow rift into the land. Its water flows only after storms. The ruins lie in the canyon on both sides of the dry riverbed. The most impressive structures were once large masonry buildings with several stories. Some have been partially restored, though others are no more than mounds.

More than 3,600 archaeological sites have been identified in the canyon.[1] They range from small shelters to dramatic multistory houses. Together, these sites tell the history of the area and its people.

People foraged wild foods in this region starting in approximately 6500 BCE. They settled in houses as early as 50 CE. Starting in the mid-800s, the people of Chaco began constructing the buildings now known as great houses. These carefully designed structures had hundreds of rooms. Many of the buildings were

Hunting was key to survival at Chaco Canyon.

oriented according to the positions of the sun and the moon. The great houses featured kivas, round underground rooms accessed by a ladder from the roof. These rooms likely served a ceremonial purpose. Small kivas at Chaco may have been used by clans or family groups. The largest might have hosted community activities for hundreds of people.

University of California, Santa Barbara anthropology professor Brian Fagan imagined what life might have been like at Chaco centuries ago:

I sensed the acrid scent of wood smoke carried on the evening breeze, dogs barking at the setting sun. Flickering hearths and blazing firebrands highlight dark windows and doorways on the terraces of the great house that is Pueblo Bonito. People move between light and shadow, dark silhouettes against the flames. The shrill cries of children playing in the shadows, the quiet talk of men leaning against sun-baked walls—the past comes alive in the gloaming.[2]

Visitors today can still sense the majesty of another era.

PRESTIGE AND POWER

The ruins flanking Chaco Wash are impressive, but the city's influence did not stop at the walls of the canyon. By 1050 CE, Chaco was the vibrant center of a culture extending 100 miles (160 km) or more in every direction. Roads connected the great houses of Chaco Canyon to more than 150 other great houses throughout the region.[3]

The power of Chaco lasted approximately 300 years. At the end of this period, people moved away

FINE ARCHITECTURE

The great houses built between 1020 and 1140 CE were not only large but also elaborately decorated. Smooth stones were carefully fitted together for the masonry, with a decorative outer layer on the walls. Craftsmen used different types of wood for different parts of the structures.

and the buildings crumbled. When archaeologists began exploring Chaco Canyon in the late 1800s, they knew nothing about the people who had lived there. They had many questions. They wanted to know who had built the impressive city, how many people had lived there, and how they had survived the desert conditions. Among the most difficult puzzles was discovering why

WHERE IS CHACO CANYON?

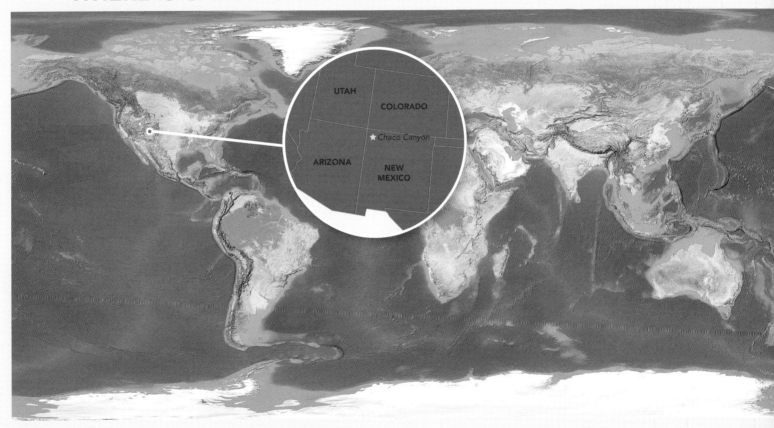

THE ANASAZI

For much of the 1900s, archaeologists referred to the ancient people of Chaco Canyon and similar sites as the Anasazi. This Navajo term means "enemy ancestors" or "ancient enemies." The Pueblo people of the Southwest, including the Hopi, are the descendants of the people of Chaco. Many feel calling their ancestors Anasazi is offensive. The word is still often used to describe the ancient people, but the preferred terms today are Ancient Pueblo or Ancestral Pueblo people.

the people eventually abandoned Chaco Canyon. Early digs only uncovered more questions. Chaco reached its peak in the early 1000s. The evidence left behind suggests people visited by the thousands but stayed for only a short time. The population feasted, left behind great wealth, constructed new buildings, and then left.

Excavations found thousands of artifacts piled high in the rooms of Chaco's great houses. Wooden staffs had handles inlaid with fine stones. Feathers and bones came from bird species living hundreds of miles away. Bear paws and mountain lion claws may have been used in ceremonies. Ceramic bowls and jars were beautifully painted. Archaeologists worked to discover whether these impressive artifacts were religious items, goods sent as taxes, items for sale, or offerings to the dead.

The early excavators had many theories about Chaco Canyon. Some thought it might be a religious center, its great houses the equivalent of churches. Others believed it was a center of government, the

Pieces of pottery, called potsherds, are among the most common artifacts found at Chaco Canyon.

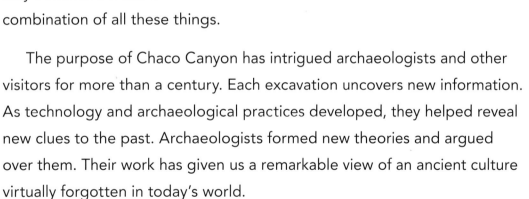

home of the ruling elite. Still others thought it might be an economic trade center or a complex to honor dead ancestors. It may even have been a combination of all these things.

The purpose of Chaco Canyon has intrigued archaeologists and other visitors for more than a century. Each excavation uncovers new information. As technology and archaeological practices developed, they helped reveal new clues to the past. Archaeologists formed new theories and argued over them. Their work has given us a remarkable view of an ancient culture virtually forgotten in today's world.

2

Exploring the Southwest

Today's Hopi and other Pueblo people are the descendants of those who lived in Chaco Canyon. Their ancestors largely left Chaco Canyon by the mid-1100s. Few people visited the region in the following centuries. Other than some Navajo who occasionally stayed in the abandoned buildings and Pueblo people who visited the site for ceremonies and rituals, only a handful of travelers passed by.

The population of Chaco Canyon declined dramatically for reasons not fully understood.

NAMING THE CANYON

The Spanish colonial name "Chaca" was used in reference to a large area of open, unexplored land. It might be a Spanish translation of a Navajo word. *Tsékoh* means "canyon" or "rock-cut," while *Tzak aih* describes a white string of rocks.

In 1849, US Army surveyor James Simpson asked Navajo, Pueblo, and Mexican guides the names of sites in Chaco Canyon. Each gave different names, and Simpson chose to use those from the Mexican guides. Many of these Spanish names are still used today, such as Casa Chiquita, or "little house," and Pueblo Bonito, or "pretty village." Other ruins have Navajo names, such as Kin Kletso, which comes from the Navajo *Kin Litso*, or "yellow house." The meanings and origins of some names have been lost to history.

At one time, the area that is now the southwestern United States belonged to Spain. A Spanish mapmaker included a location labeled as "Chaca" on a 1774 map. However, he probably did not visit the ruins and only recorded what local guides told him.

In 1822, Mexican colonists rebelled against Spain, and Mexico became a free nation. At the time, Mexico controlled the territory that is now New Mexico, Arizona, Colorado, Utah, Texas, and California. A unit of the Mexican military passed through Chaco Canyon in 1823, when New Mexico was a Mexican province. The governor of New Mexico made note of the ruins, but the group did not linger to explore.

By the mid-1800s, a few more outsiders were beginning to stumble upon Chaco Canyon. Popular author Josiah Gregg mentioned the Chaco pueblos in an 1844 book. He described the ruins as the work of people descended from the Aztecs. This was a popular—and incorrect—belief at the time. This shows how little nonnative people knew about the area and its former inhabitants.

In 1846, the United States went to war with Mexico in an attempt to gain territory. After its victory in the Mexican-American War (1846–1848), the United States took possession of what is now nearly the entire southwestern United States. In 1849, US Army surveyors explored Chaco Canyon with the help of Native American guides. They

The Mexican-American War brought Chaco Canyon into US territory, opening the way for US archaeologists to explore it.

THE NAVAJO AT CHACO

Navajo people live in the area around Chaco today, and many of the ruins are known by Navajo names. Some Navajo say their legends connect them to the building of Chaco. However, the Navajo people probably did not enter the region until after Chaco was abandoned.

wrote detailed notes and sketched some of the ruins during their short visit. Now that New Mexico was a US territory, Chaco Canyon became part of the United States.

Popular photographer William Henry Jackson traveled to Chaco Canyon to photograph the ruins in 1877. He experimented with a new film process, but it failed. He lost the photographs, but he still returned with notes about his visit. In 1888, two men from the Smithsonian Museum, Victor and Cosmos Mindeleff, spent several weeks at Chaco. They surveyed the sites and took the first successful photographs of the canyon's ruins. The public was starting to hear more about these mysterious ruins. The site intrigued everyone who passed through, yet none of these visitors conducted in-depth examinations of Chaco Canyon.

AN AMATEUR DIGS IN

One of the first explorers to thoroughly investigate Chaco Canyon was Richard Wetherill. The Wetherill family owned a ranch in southwestern Colorado, and Richard often explored the region when not busy with ranching duties. In 1888, Richard and his brother-in-law were searching for stray cattle in a snowstorm. They stumbled across the ancient ruins of Mesa Verde in southwestern Colorado. They spent several hours exploring the ruins, and Richard's interest in archaeology grew.

The Wetherill family began collecting artifacts and guiding tourists to nearby archeological sites. One of these visitors was Swedish collector Gustav Nordenskiöld. He taught the Wetherills advanced European archaeology techniques. Nordenskiöld later took a large collection of southwestern artifacts, mostly from Mesa Verde, to Sweden. No laws prevented the selling or export of these items, but some Americans complained about the artifacts leaving the country. Archaeology was a relatively new field, but concern for protecting the past was growing.

In October 1895, Richard Wetherill met a visiting family, the Palmers, who were also interested in archaeology. Wetherill and the Palmers traveled to Chaco Canyon. Since Chaco Canyon was so remote, they had to bring all supplies with them for their expedition. They carried approximately 1,000 pounds (450 kg) of food for the people and an equal weight of hay and grain for their animals. They carried barrels of water and bedding for sleeping in the wagons or on the ground. Four mules pulled two wagons full of supplies. They also brought along three horses. Eighteen-year-old Marietta Palmer wrote about the journey to Chaco Canyon in her diary: "No road except

RICHARD WETHERILL

Richard Wetherill, born in 1858, was the oldest of five cowboy brothers. His family moved from Kansas to Colorado in the early 1880s. Besides ranching, they explored prehistoric ruins in the area. Although he had no professional training as an archaeologist, Richard made many important finds. He did his greatest work at Chaco Canyon, although he faced much criticism. He agreed to give up his claim to the lands there if the government would take over the ruins and protect them, which happened in 1907. Richard continued operating a trading post nearby until his death. In 1910, he was murdered in a fight over a stolen horse.

Wetherill opened a trading post against the walls of Pueblo Bonito.

Mesa Verde was an early target of Wetherill's archaeological interests.

the old unknown road [used] by early explorers to San Juan from Santa Fe. Many places so grass grown we could not find it. Other places entirely washed out."[1]

The group spent a month exploring. During this visit, Richard fell in love with Marietta, and they eventually married. He also fell in love with Chaco Canyon. The exploration of the site would become his life's work.

Wetherill wanted more time to dig at Chaco, but he could not afford to do the work without pay. He wrote to the Hyde brothers, wealthy New Yorkers who sometimes provided financial support for excavations. The Hydes agreed to fund a dig at Chaco Canyon. In return, the artifacts and records would go to the American Museum of Natural History in New York City.

The Hydes wanted the expedition to be taken seriously, so they hired Frederic Putnam, an archaeologist from the museum, to lead the expedition. However, Putnam remained in New York and sent his assistant, George Pepper, to the actual site. Pepper had no formal archaeological training or experience, and Wetherill did not get along with him. Despite their differences, they conducted a successful dig in 1896 with the help of local Navajo workers.

The team searched for burials and trash mounds. These archaeological features would most likely provide valuable artifacts the ancient people had left behind. They also dug out the

SELLING ARTIFACTS

The United States did not have laws in place to protect artifacts until the early 1900s. Before that, digging in ruins and selling the artifacts was a generally accepted practice. Even professional archaeologists worked without permits and sold their finds. In an 1894 issue of *Archaeologist* magazine, the editor criticized "vandals" who "failed to record their observations." But he also said, "The sale of a whole collection, or part of it, so long as complete finds are not split, is always proper. Single specimens, bought of dealers, may be sold with a free conscience, also complete finds. What is really wrong is the destruction of scientific testimony."[2]

dirt filling some of the ruins' rooms. Their excavation of a great house called Pueblo Bonito provided spectacular results. The semicircular stone structure featured more than 600 rooms.[3] In the first season, the team dug out 37 rooms and collected enough artifacts to fill a railroad freight car. In a single room, they found 114 clay jars and 22 bowls. Nearby rooms held carved human figures and wooden wands. A basket covered with a turquoise mosaic held thousands of beads and pendants made of turquoise and shells. The dig continued, uncovering amazing finds over several seasons. But trouble was brewing.

CONFLICT AND CRITICISM

In the late 1800s, archaeology was a relatively new science, especially in the United States. Wetherill had no official training when he began exploring ruins in the Southwest. Still, he took his work seriously. Many early "pothunters" sold artifacts to individual collectors, destroying countless archaeological sites in the process. The items were then unavailable for study by experts. Wetherill did this for only a short time

REVERSE ARCHAEOLOGY

Modern archaeologists are often frustrated by poor record keeping from those who worked in the early years of the profession. Yet sometimes lost records can be rediscovered. In the 1980s, a group of people, mainly amateur archaeologists, launched the Wetherill-Grand Gulch Research Project. They discovered many of Wetherill's notes still existed, along with dozens of his photographs. Project members managed to find some lost dig sites based on vague written clues. They also began trying to link the notes to museum artifacts. Pairing notes with the correct items could bring new information to light.

before deciding it was wrong. Then he began selling his finds to museums where they could be studied.

Wetherill attempted to excavate as scientifically as possible, based on his limited knowledge of the practices of the time. His letter to the Hyde brothers telling them about Chaco Canyon shows his serious interest: "I am saving specimens from all over this region for comparative study. I have voluminous notes of this trip, a copy of which I will send you."[4] Unfortunately, many of his notes were lost, ignored, misinterpreted, or separated from the artifacts they described.

Wetherill was also responsible for some decisions that damaged the site. In 1898, he built a trading post against the back wall of Pueblo Bonito. Wetherill's son, Richard Wetherill II, described it in a 1978 interview:

> *The first store in Chaco Canyon was in [a] ruin at Pueblo Bonito. The first room was the store and part of the kitchen. To enlarge it they had cut some doorways into the little dark rooms with the beautiful ceilings smoked up. In there is where they had a bedroom and in front was the store.[5]*

Pueblo Bonito was once the largest great house at Chaco Canyon, but time reduced much of it to rubble.

Actions like this drew the ire of other archaeologists and officials. The criticism may have been partly political, as some of the critics wanted to do their own work at the canyon. The government launched two investigations into the dig. Though they found nothing illegal, the government suspended excavations in 1901.

PRESERVING OUR PAST

American archaeology got a boost on June 8, 1906, with the enactment of the Act for the Preservation of American Antiquities. It made disturbing a historic or prehistoric ruin on public land a federal crime. The act also allowed the US president, acting alone, to protect public areas for historical or scientific purposes. Prior to the act, Congress had to be involved as well. The law was strengthened in 1979 with the passage of the Archaeological Resources Protection Act. The new act allowed only those with proper permits to conduct archaeological digs on government land. While some people still dig illegally, the law helps preserve important sites for trained archaeologists. Other laws provide protection for sites on private land.

The publicity surrounding Richard Wetherill's activities helped lead to new laws protecting ancient sites. The Act for the Preservation of American Antiquities was passed in 1906. On March 11, 1907, President Theodore Roosevelt created the Chaco Canyon National Monument. The proclamation referred to the ruins' "extraordinary interest because of their number and their great size and because of the innumerable and valuable relics of a prehistoric people which they contain."[6] Five years later, on January 6, 1912, New Mexico was granted statehood as the forty-seventh member of the United States.

Richard and Marietta Wetherill stayed in Chaco Canyon even though he could no longer dig there. They operated the trading post in a new building until Richard's death in 1910. Richard Wetherill II grew up in Chaco. He remembered, "I used to play in the north part of Bonito and there were lots of hiding places, but they filled in all those rooms. We played hide and seek and everything else all over the place, but it was darn hard to find anybody! We went in every hole we could find."[7]

Even today, archaeologists hold mixed opinions about Richard Wetherill. However, most now agree he did as well as other excavators of the time. Wetherill certainly did not get rich from his archaeological work. He once wrote to the Hydes, "I started from home dead broke and am still that way but have not yet missed a meal. I love the work and the research and for that reason I can stand almost anything."[8]

3

Searching for Clues

In 1921, the National Geographic Society sent an expedition to work at Chaco Canyon. Neil Judd of the Smithsonian Institution led the dig. His team consisted largely of college students studying archaeology, alongside local Navajo and Zuni workers. They spent five years excavating and stabilizing Pueblo Bonito, alternating between four months in the field and eight months of museum work.

Expeditions in the 1920s showed there was still much to learn about Chaco Canyon, even in the areas already thought to be fully explored.

The team lived ruggedly during the months spent in the field. Judd wrote:

The first season's party pitched its tents on the adobe flat before the famous ruin early in May 1921, improvised for its kitchen stove an altogether inadequate shelter from spring sandstorms, dug a well in the nearby arroyo, and went to work.[1]

TENSIONS IN THE FIELD

In the early 1900s, archaeologists and institutions often fought over intriguing sites. Some western archaeologists resented those who came from big East Coast museums. Meanwhile, eastern archaeologists who had developed new excavation techniques deplored the sloppy methods they saw in the West. The rivalries extended to major museums such as the American Museum of Natural History in New York and the Smithsonian Institution in Washington, DC. In order to conduct a dig, a group needed both funding and permission, which required political support. Archaeologists had to convince museums their planned digs were in areas worthy of study.

Judd called Pueblo Bonito the largest apartment house in the world built before the 1880s. He thought a peak of perhaps 1,000 people lived there during its heyday.[2] He saw the walls of Pueblo Bonito as defensive fortifications. To him, this suggested wandering raiders must have been a threat to Chaco.

One of Judd's most impressive finds at Pueblo Bonito, an ornate necklace, was uncovered almost by accident. Judd was working near an area he thought had been cleared. He wrote:

> The second stroke of my trowel on a floor already swept with hand brooms brought several beads to light. A few moments more with awl and brush and there lay a carefully coiled turquoise necklace. . . . I cannot adequately describe the thrill of that discovery. . . . A casual scrape of a trowel across the ash-strewn floor, a stroke as mechanical as a thousand other strokes made every day, exposed the long-hidden treasure.[3]

After excavating Pueblo Bonito, Judd surveyed the nearby ancient roads. These seemed to go only short distances from the canyon. Judd thought they might have been used to transport tree trunks. This wood was needed for roof beams and lintels, the horizontal supports across the tops of doors or windows.

Judd's team tried to find the source of the wood used in building Pueblo Bonito. They found only a few dozen trees within 16 miles (26 km) of the ruin. Yet thousands of logs had been used. Judd noted, "They had been felled and peeled while green; they showed no scars of transportation. Clearly they were cut within easy carrying distance."[4] He assumed this meant Chaco Canyon had more rainfall and healthy forests at the time of its occupation.

WHERE ARE THE WOODS?

The Chaco architects used wooden beams for roofs and support lintels. More than 25,000 pine roof beams were used in Pueblo Bonito alone.[5] Other Chaco ruins were nearly as large and had similar construction. By some estimates, 225,000 trees were used in the buildings of Chaco Canyon. It appeared these trees did not grow locally, as no forests grow in the canyon today. Some believe the area was once rainier and lusher, with more sources of trees. Others contend the wood was brought in from mountain forests 60 miles (100 km) away.[6]

Many of these logs were 15 feet (5 m) long and 9 inches (22 cm) in diameter. Each one weighed approximately 600 pounds (275 kg).[7] The Ancestral Pueblo moved these large trees without wheeled vehicles or animal power.

He thought people must have cut the trees, leading to erosion which made it hard to control floodwaters. In turn, this could have led to failed crops and the abandonment of the canyon.

TRACKING TIME

Judd tried to figure out when various buildings at Chaco had been constructed by comparing building styles. Early buildings were small and simple, with walls only one stone thick. Later, great houses had walls with a core of rubble and an outer veneer of thin pieces of sandstone. The final style used a thin rubble core and a thicker outer layer.

Judd's team also studied pottery in order to determine when the Chaco buildings were used. Pottery styles change over time, so archaeologists can use ceramics to identify the age of a site. This technique is easier to use at more recent European sites, because European pottery manufacturers kept records on the ceramics they produced starting in the late 1500s. Many manufacturers also marked their ceramics with their names. With these records, archaeologists can often get a specific date for a piece of pottery.

Southwestern pottery does not have these marks or records. Still, archaeologists learned to identify the changes over time. The materials used to make and temper the pottery vary.

Transporting logs was a labor-intensive task for a society that had not invented the wheel.

The shape of the vessel, surface texture, and painting styles also identify specific time periods. Even small fragments of pottery, called potsherds, can identify a particular era. Ceramics also show regional variations. If pottery from a faraway region is found, it could indicate foreign people had visited or immigrated.

DATING TECHNIQUES

Archaeologists use several methods to determine the age of a site. Stratigraphy looks at the layers of a site. Older artifacts are usually found below younger ones. Style analysis compares artifacts to other items with known dates. Pottery, stoneware, glass, metal objects, and architectural styles change over time. If a certain style is known to be from a specific time period, items of that style are assumed to be from the same time. Relative dating requires knowledge of when one artifact was made. Artifacts found nearby might be assumed to have a similar age.

These techniques are all flawed and only give rough dates. Several absolute dating techniques using laboratory analysis are more accurate. Radiocarbon dating can determine how old organic matter is. Uranium-lead dating can do the same for stone items. These techniques can typically give a specific date, but they may damage or destroy the object in the process.

For his studies, Judd collected pottery fragments from Pueblo Bonito's trash mounds. During the years of the investigation, his team uncovered thousands of potsherds. They also uncovered a mystery. His team began digging in a trash mound near the Pueblo, uncovering layers of potsherds. They expected to find the oldest potsherds at the bottom and newer potsherds at the top of the mound. This would reflect the order in which they had been thrown away. However, they found the reverse: the newer potsherds on the bottom and the oldest on the top. Excavations into a second trash mound found the same pattern.

ANCIENT POTTERY

Pottery probably appeared in the Southwest around 200 CE. By the early 500s, pots were widely used. The Ancestral Pueblos mixed wet clay with crushed rock, sand, or crushed pottery. Potters rolled this mixture into long strands and then coiled the strands around a base to build up the sides of a pot. The coils were smoothed into walls, and then the pot was dried and fired.

Early potters made bowls and jars in simple shapes. Later people sometimes made vessels in unusual shapes, such as gourds or ducks. They began using black paint from plant juices or mineral pigments. Over time, potters developed a greater variety of shapes, textures, and designs.

This problem left the team baffled. They finally suspected a trash mound had been dug out in the past and turned upside down as it was moved. They found evidence of this in further excavations. A trash mound had been dug out in order to build an underground room. When the trash was moved, the top layer was deposited at the new site first. As older layers were dug up, they were piled on top.

PRESERVING RUINS

In the early 1900s, ancient ruins, including those found at Chaco, were sometimes repaired. Crews patched walls with replacement building stones in hopes of preventing further deterioration. Today, however, archaeologists consider it inappropriate to rebuild or restore ancient sites. Instead, the National Park Service, which is in charge of Chaco Canyon today, tries to prevent additional damage. Some buildings are simply left in unexcavated mounds so the upper layers of rubble preserve the structures underneath.

Fortunately, Judd's team already knew enough about pottery styles to catch the unusual situation. Surprises like this demonstrate why archaeologists should not make quick assumptions about what they find.

MAKING PROGRESS

Judd's team made important discoveries at Pueblo Bonito and contributed to a greater understanding of the Ancestral Pueblo people. Judd's team also tried to preserve the portions of Pueblo Bonito they excavated. They strengthened walls, patched broken masonry, replaced missing door lintels, and repaired vandalized walls.

To best understand a site, archaeologists need broad knowledge about the surrounding region and the cultures found there. While work was going on at Chaco, other archaeologists were excavating different Southwestern sites. The information uncovered helped lead to a better understanding of Chaco Canyon and the Pueblo people of the past.

In 1927, 40 archaeologists met at an informal conference in New Mexico. They tried to organize a system of nomenclature so everyone would be using the same terms. The group also identified eight stages of civilization for the ancient people. While they had some mistaken ideas about the Ancestral Pueblo people, this helped push the study of Southwestern archaeology forward.

In the early 1900s, Chaco Canyon archaeologists still had more questions than answers. Were the great houses at Chaco truly apartment buildings? By some estimates, if all the rooms had been occupied at once, approximately 10,000 people would have lived in the canyon. Researchers struggled to understand how such a large population could survive in the desert.

Despite many impressive finds, archaeologists had studied only a tiny portion of the buildings which once filled Chaco Canyon. To learn more about the Ancestral Pueblo people, they needed to search beyond the most impressive ruins.

STILL MEETING

The 1927 archaeology conference was known as the Pecos Conference. It was named for its location in Pecos Pueblo, New Mexico. The conference became an annual event, and Southwest archaeologists continue to meet each summer to share research and discuss challenges. It is still called the Pecos Conference, but the meeting place moves around throughout the southwestern United States and northwestern Mexico.

4

Beyond Pueblo Bonito

Attitudes about archaeology were changing in the first half of the 1900s. It was no longer enough to find glamorous treasures. Researchers wanted to understand how the subjects of their study lived on a daily basis. This meant studying the ruins of everyday life in addition to more high-profile grave goods and other unusual finds.

As work continued at Chaco Canyon, archaeologists moved outward to smaller sites. Among these was Pueblo del Arroyo, the only site at Chaco with triple-walled construction.

These new ideals encouraged Chaco Canyon archaeologists to go beyond the big ruins, such as Pueblo Bonito. A new wave of students studying archaeology provided skilled researchers for this effort. One important figure was Edgar Lee Hewett, a professor of archaeology at the University of New Mexico. He had been active in Southwestern archaeology for decades and was instrumental in the passage of the 1906 Antiquities Act. In 1936, he established a summer field school at Chaco Canyon for his students. Some of his graduate students did important work there, mainly focusing on small sites.

Students Gordon Vivian and Janet Woods excavated a great kiva called Casa Rinconada. This site is located on

THE KIVA

Kivas, common features in Ancestral Pueblo sites, are rooms set belowground. The circular Chaco kivas are entered using ladders. They have benches along the inside wall, fire pits, and a small hole called a *sipapu* near the center of the room. *Sipapu* is a Hopi word referring to the place where the mythical first inhabitants of the world climbed up a hollow reed into a hole in the sky.

Modern kivas are used for men's ceremonial groups in today's pueblos. Hewett strongly promoted the idea that ancient kivas also served religious and ceremonial functions. This idea went largely unchallenged for decades, but now some experts suspect they might have been political meeting houses or community centers.

Casa Rinconada's great kiva is not connected to a larger group of structures in the way the kivas at Pueblo Bonito and most other sites are.

top of a ridge across the canyon from Pueblo Bonito, among a cluster of small house sites. Casa Rinconada is a circular structure, with an interior diameter of approximately 63 feet (19 m). It is partially underground and has a 39-foot- (12 m) long underground passage leading into it. The passage might have allowed people to appear suddenly and dramatically during ceremonies. Vivian and Woods uncovered beads, pendants, and ceramics during their excavations. Although the artifacts were not especially impressive, excavations like this gave insight into the Chaco way of life.

THREATENING ROCK FALLS

Preserving and protecting ancient ruins is not always possible. A huge slab of rock on the cliff behind it threatened Pueblo Bonito. The Ancestral Pueblo had jammed logs beneath it and built up platforms and buttresses for support. The National Park Service was concerned the slab, known as Threatening Rock, would fall on Pueblo Bonito. They removed some of the sand and rocks piled up behind the slab, hoping to relieve the weight. Still, on January 22, 1941, Threatening Rock collapsed. Approximately 65 rooms were destroyed in the avalanche of stone that fell upon Pueblo Bonito.[1]

Vivian went on to have a lifelong career as a National Park Service archaeologist at Chaco Canyon. He lived with his wife and children in a traditional stone-walled Navajo-style house near the Casa Rinconada ruin.

During his time with the National Park Service, Vivian developed new techniques for protecting the ruins. These included building stabilizing walls and diverting water that could cause damage. In one case, an emergency repair led to a new discovery. Flooding weakened the wall of a first-story room at a ruin called Chetro Ketl. Vivian decided to remove the debris filling the room above it in order to lessen the weight on the lower walls. Excavators removed part of a collapsed roof in the second-story room. Underneath, they found 200 carved and painted wooden artifacts that had been protected by a six-inch (15 cm) layer of sand and silt. Some of the wands and staffs still had their original painted decorations.

These finds were exciting, but Vivian was curious about more mundane elements of Chaco as well.

He became interested in the agriculture of the Ancestral Pueblo people. He did some initial studies investigating how the ancient people controlled soil and water. His son Gwinn played around the ruins as a child and would later continue his father's work.

LEARNING FROM TREES

Women were entering the field of archaeology in greater numbers at this time. One of Hewett's students, Florence Hawley, studied pottery at the canyon. She was also a pioneer in dendrochronology, the practice of using tree rings to date archaeological sites. After her time as a student, she spent an additional 11 seasons at Chaco Canyon, focusing on excavations and tree-ring research and directing laboratory work.

Using wood samples to date dig sites shows how far archaeology had progressed in only a few decades. When Wetherill's team found burned wood, they reused it in their campfires. They did not see wood fragments as having any value and were only interested in complete artifacts. They did not realize the wood could have provided later archaeologists with invaluable information through tree-ring dating.

Hawley's tree-ring dating work benefited her pottery studies. She used dates from samples of wood to date the pottery found there. She could then compare that pottery with samples from other settlements.

DIGGING
DEEPER

Dendrochronology

Determining exactly when a site was active has been a challenge for archaeologists. One method is dendrochronology, which uses tree rings from a particular area. Cross sections of trees show annual growth rings, which vary depending on the temperatures and amount of rain each year. By looking at the rings in a living tree, one can see growth patterns from recent decades. These can be compared with rings from an older tree. If some areas overlap, one can create a tree-ring record of past climate changes.

Astronomer A. E. Douglass developed dendrochronology. He was interested in the links between solar activity and global climate change. He had the idea to collect tree ring samples and compare the patterns. By 1915, he had a chronology of growth rings from

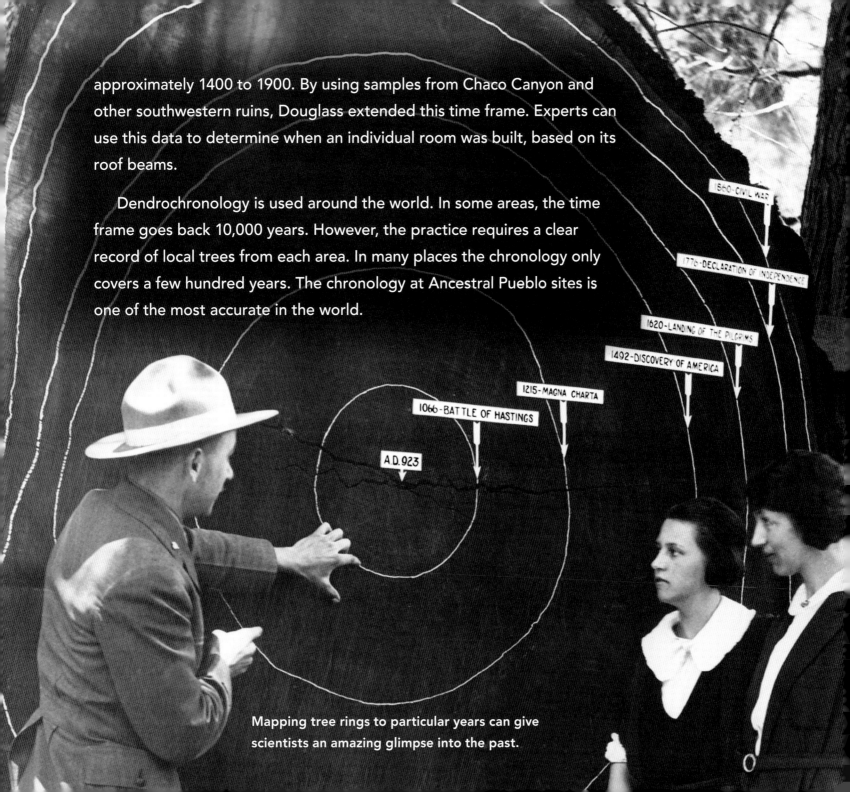

approximately 1400 to 1900. By using samples from Chaco Canyon and other southwestern ruins, Douglass extended this time frame. Experts can use this data to determine when an individual room was built, based on its roof beams.

Dendrochronology is used around the world. In some areas, the time frame goes back 10,000 years. However, the practice requires a clear record of local trees from each area. In many places the chronology only covers a few hundred years. The chronology at Ancestral Pueblo sites is one of the most accurate in the world.

1860-CIVIL WAR

1776-DECLARATION OF INDEPENDENCE

1620-LANDING OF THE PILGRIMS

1492-DISCOVERY OF AMERICA

1215-MAGNA CHARTA

1066-BATTLE OF HASTINGS

A.D.923

Mapping tree rings to particular years can give scientists an amazing glimpse into the past.

In the early days of dendrochronology, people compared tree rings visually. Since then, the study of tree rings has gotten more detailed, and technology allows researchers to study microscopic sections. By using X-rays, scientists can determine the maximum and minimum densities within each ring. Dense areas indicate slower growth. Computer software processes images, saving time and preventing human error.

Hawley developed a system for classifying pottery and published a manual on Southwestern ceramics.

Chaco grew over time, so to truly understand the culture, archaeologists needed to see what happened at each stage of its development. They focused on when exactly different structures had been built. Several techniques helped them date the buildings. Pottery samples found in trash heaps helped identify when buildings were used. Tree-ring dating of rafters provided an even better record of when structures were built. Roof beam tree rings also provided archaeologists with a record of climate. The rings showed a pattern of rainy years and drought that seemed to coincide with the ups and downs of life at Chaco.

Another clue for archaeologists was how the type of wood used at Chaco changed over time. Before 950, builders used mostly trees that grew fairly nearby,

Agriculture alone at Chaco Canyon likely did not provide enough food to support the growing population.

DRY LAND

The climate of northwestern New Mexico is harsh now, just as it was 1,000 years ago. Richard Wetherill II described the variability of water in the canyon in the early 1900s:

> We had a shallow well down in the arroyo off just to one side from the main channel, right in front of the ruin. . . . We had to get all our water out of that well. There was no other water around except for those springs up in the canyons. When it rained there was a lot of water that come down that wash in floods, but it never did hurt anything.[2]

such as piñon, juniper, and cottonwood. After 950, ponderosa predominated; it had to be brought in from mountains more than 50 miles (80 km) away. By 1030, the people of Chaco had to use fir and spruce from higher in the mountains. Their ability to gather wood from these distant sources demonstrates Chaco's importance and its growing workforce.

From the accumulating evidence, archaeologists guessed at the history of Chaco. The region around Chaco was never ideal for farming, but the people could survive occasional dry periods. They simply used more wild food and foods they had stored during good years. However, as Chaco grew larger, it also grew more vulnerable. The communities needed so much food they had to import some. People also needed an enormous amount of wood, since it was used for building, for firewood, and for firing clay pots. Pottery was necessary for carrying water, storing food, and cooking.

By approximately 1000, the local forests were gone, and trees had to be hauled in from distant mountain forests. Pottery was also imported so it did not need to be made locally. The people of Chaco may even have imported much of their grain. Chaco had become the center of a great trading network, but the cost of this power was the loss of self-sufficiency.

A major drought began in approximately 1130 and lasted for 50 years. Crops failed, wild plants also died off, and storerooms emptied. Chaco was probably not abandoned quickly, and the drought likely did not kill a large number of people. Instead, over the course of a generation, families began moving away. By 1150, Chaco was largely abandoned. Neighboring communities grew larger and more important.

Evidence gathered at the site led archaeologists to believe they knew how Chaco had grown and why it ultimately failed. Yet the story was not complete.

5

The Chaco Project

By the 1960s, archaeologists had a long list of questions about Chaco. John Corbett, chief archaeologist for the National Park Service, organized a team of archaeologists to address these questions. Corbett had worked at Chaco as a university student. He knew a great deal of information lay hidden in the canyon, discoverable only through comprehensive surveys, excavations, and artifact analysis.

The Chaco Project was the first attempt to systematically gather data from the entire range of sites at Chaco Canyon.

THE ANCIENT DIET

Before approximately 700, the people of Chaco depended on hunting and gathering for most of their food. They used spears with large stone points. Atlatls, or spear throwers, provided extra power. After 700, people began switching to bows and arrows with small stone points. These are ideal for hunting small mammals and birds such as rabbits, prairie dogs, and turkeys. People also depended more on agriculture. Corn, beans, and squash were the dominant plant foods. Archaeologists have also found watermelon seeds and piñon shells from pine nuts.

Putting together such a project was not easy. It required funding and cooperation between the park, the government, and research groups. After more than five years of negotiations, the Chaco Project finally began in 1970. It started with a survey of all the land within the park boundary. This survey identified almost 4,000 sites, ranging from prehistoric sites to modern-day Navajo settlements. The project collected more than 100,000 artifacts from the surface of approximately 1,800 sites.[1] These artifacts were mainly potsherds and stone items. The team also took photographs, drew maps, and took detailed notes.

After this initial survey, the Chaco Project went on to excavate 70 sites.[2] They chose sites from different time periods and from areas used for different purposes. These excavations were designed to help archaeologists answer specific questions. When were these sites built and how long were they occupied? What kind of work did the people do? What did they eat? What was community life like? Corbett's colleague, Wilfred Logan, wrote, "John never forgot that he was dealing with things human. He was vibrantly aware that these things came from people who lived, ate, starved, became angry, fought each other, loved, married, produced children, died, and were grieved for."[3]

More than 430,000 artifacts were collected.[4] Researchers found everything from ceramic vessels and bone tools to samples of soil and pollen. The dry climate that challenged the people of Chaco benefited the archaeologists. Many artifacts survived that might have rotted away in wetter climates. Dry caves offered additional protection from the elements. Fragile items such as sandals, mats, and wooden drills used to start fires were preserved. Even samples of cord and string survived through the centuries. Cord was made from cotton, human hair, fibers from the yucca plant, animal sinew, and animal fur. Fur string was sometimes twined with turkey feathers to create blankets.

Artifacts like these gave an in-depth look at Chaco life. Studies of soil chemistry

The artifacts at Chaco included stone tools used to grind seeds and grains for food.

and ancient pollen samples offered clues to the ancient diet.

VIEW FROM ABOVE

Collecting artifacts and mapping sites has always been the basis of modern archaeological excavation. However, the Chaco Project went beyond ground surveys and excavations. The National Environmental Policy Act required all federal agencies to assess the effect their actions would have on the environment. Archaeological excavations changed a site and could even destroy it as material was removed. Future generations might have more advanced archaeology techniques. These would be useless without untouched sites to study. Many experts started feeling some sites should be preserved for future research. The concept of conservation archaeology arose. Instead of completely excavating a site, archaeologists would try to understand it without disturbing it.

Fortunately, technological advances allowed researchers to see Chaco Canyon in new ways.

STUDYING POLLEN

Palynology refers to the science of studying pollen samples. Pollen may be found embedded in artifacts such as pots. It can also be found in ancient, dried human feces, known to archaeologists as coprolites. Pollen can be used to trace the history of certain plants, showing when they were domesticated. It can also indicate which foods were most common in the ancient diet. Starting in the 1950s, pollen was analyzed from many archaeological sites in the Southwest.

Remote-sensing exploration consists of various methods of studying a site from a distance. Aerial photography is one way to do this. Photographs taken from the air clearly show the network of roads connecting Chaco to other sites.

Another technique is airborne laser scanning, which uses a laser beam to measure the distance between the airplane and the ground. This can reveal archaeological detail even when it is hidden underneath dense forests. Aerial studies like these confirmed the existence of a large network of roads.

EARLY PEOPLE

The great culture of Chaco did not spring from nothing. People known as the Basketmakers lived in the Southwest starting as early as 7,000 years ago. Through excavations, archaeologists have learned the Basketmakers were dependent on maize agriculture by 500 BCE. Farming led to more permanent settlements. The Basketmaker people are known for new forms of basketry and for homes called pit houses. Styles of pit houses varied, but they are typically circular with a fire pit in the center. They were partially underground, but could be shallow or deep. Two large pit house villages in Chaco Canyon show the canyon has been important for many centuries. One is on the mesa some nine miles (14 km) from Pueblo Bonito. It may have contained approximately 60 pit houses, plus stone storage boxes, a paved courtyard, and a great kiva.[5] Many archaeologists believe the pit house may have evolved into the kiva.

DIGGING
DEEPER

Remote Sensing

Technology allows archaeologists to see beneath the ground's surface without digging. Different kinds of rock, soil, sand, and vegetation have different temperatures and emit heat at different rates. Special sensors can pick up on these subtle differences and identify various substances.

Loose soil may indicate a prehistoric agricultural field or burial site. Buried stone buildings may show up because stone is slightly warmer than the surrounding terrain. Buried archaeological features can also affect how plants grow above them, which can help archaeologists identify those features without digging.

Remote controlled
drones can be used
for precision aerial
photography.

Several remote-sensing devices and methods are
available to archaeologists. Aerial photography provides a new
perspective on large ruins. Color infrared film detects slight differences
in vegetation, showing areas where buried features have impacted plant growth.
With airborne lidar, researchers fire a laser out of an airplane down to the ground.
The time it takes for the beam to bounce back is processed to provide tree height,
surface details, and even water depth. More than 400 laser beams are shot per
second to provide a highly detailed map.

The Chaco Project's Remote Sensing Division produced maps of this road system. This created new interest in cities connected to Chaco by trade.

RESOURCES AND RECORDS

Not all aspects of the Chaco Project depended on advanced technology. Ethnographic studies focused on the customs of modern Native Americans in the region. Pueblo consultants examined artifacts and suggested interpretations. Tools, household goods, and building styles of today might have had similar uses in Ancestral Pueblo times.

Oral histories documented the knowledge of living people. Migration legends suggested the possible history of Chaco Canyon. Researchers also looked for documents and photographs from Navajo and European settlers of recent centuries. These records helped fill in gaps between the prehistoric era and modern studies.

Other specialists worked in many different fields. A team surveyed the rock art around the canyon. Tree-ring data collection continued. Studies of burials gave insight into the people who once lived at Chaco. By studying skeletons, experts can determine the gender and age at death, as well as any diseases or injuries the person might have had. These studies led to an enormous increase in knowledge about Chaco Canyon and its ancient people.

Some excavators at other sites had collected huge amounts of materials but then did little with the information. Half-written reports and uncataloged artifacts do nothing to expand knowledge. Those in charge of the Chaco Project were determined to see the material properly published. The Chaco Center produced more than 20 volumes on the project's work. They covered topics such as architecture, ceramics, history, settlement patterns, and remote-sensing techniques. Advances in digital technology also made it easier to store and retrieve data. The Chaco Project introduced a computerized database, which provided easier access to all the new research.

STAGES OF THE ANCESTRAL PUEBLO

Archaeologists have identified several stages of Ancestral Pueblo civilization.

- 6500–1200 BCE, Archaic period: People forage for wild foods and hunt with the atlatl or dart.

- 1200 BCE–50 CE, Early Basketmaker II: Caves are used for camping, storage, and burial. People cultivate corn and squash.

- 50–500, Late Basketmaker II: People begin using shallow pit houses and storage pits.

- 500–750, Basketmaker III: The bow and arrow replace the atlatl. Beans are added to the diet and people begin using pottery.

- 750–900, Pueblo I: Large villages with blocks of rooms arise in some areas. Pottery develops with more styles.

- 900–1150, Pueblo II: Chaco blooms with great houses, kivas, and roads to nearby communities. The Chaco system declines around 1140.

Information from the Chaco Project also helped park managers make decisions about resource management. This is the practice of making efficient and effective use of an organization's resources, such as labor, equipment, and funding. The project even led to a law recognizing the importance of Chaco Canyon and encouraging protection and further research.

MAKING SENSE OF IT ALL

As researchers learned more about Chaco, new ideas developed about the population. Earlier archaeologists assumed the large buildings were the equivalent of apartments. With so many rooms, they figured surely thousands of people had lived at Chaco at once. However, the data did not always support that conclusion. Only 131 skeletons were found at Pueblo Bonito, and only 650 were present in the entire canyon. Despite its vast size and 700 rooms, Pueblo Bonito had only enough kitchen hearths for approximately 70 people.[6] The early Wetherill and Judd excavations had found many domestic

"I heard the blare of shell trumpets during festivals, ceremonies, and feasts. During years of good rains and robust harvests, travelers would have come by the thousands, their baskets loaded with corn and with beautifully rendered trinkets, the finest of their wares brought from home to leave here. Feathered dancers would have made a sound like sea waves crashing against the shore, their feet pounding, their kilts and ankles loud with shell tinklers."[7]

—WRITER CRAIG CHILDS IMAGINING LIFE AT CHACO CANYON

artifacts, including between 1,000 and 2,000 vessels.[8] Yet excavators found very little of the debris one would expect from day-to-day living inside the buildings. Instead of charcoal and potsherds, they found stacks of painted bowls and feathers from macaws and golden eagles.

Many theories tried to make sense of new findings. Archaeologists are like detectives working to piece together clues. They can interpret the evidence, but they rarely know for certain what happened centuries ago. Multiple answers may be correct if a place changed over time. Perhaps in the early days, the structures at Chaco were homes. They may have taken on different functions in later times.

The research at Chaco reflected a change in attitude among archaeologists. Instead of focusing on excavations at a single site, people began studying the entire cultural landscape. As anthropologist Brian Fagan wrote, "We now know that the story of Chaco cannot be told simply by studying its great houses and small settlements. Much of the story lies far beyond the canyon walls."[9]

Descendants of the Ancient Pueblos still return to Pueblo Bonito for ceremonial dances.

6

Water and Roads

Gordon Vivian was one of the first people to describe the Chaco water control system. In the 1960s and 1970s, Gwinn Vivian continued his father's work by exploring Chaco's ancient irrigation systems. He used aerial photographs to identify 25 separate drainage areas on the north side of Chaco Canyon. From these places, the water was channeled down the sides of the mesa.

Early expeditions to Chaco recognized the importance of controlling the area's unpredictable water.

Chaco does not seem like a good choice for large settlements if people had to grow all their own food. The canyon is near the center of the San Juan Basin, a relatively flat region between high mountains. Summer temperatures rise to more than 90 degrees Fahrenheit (32°C). Winters are cold, with temperatures dropping below freezing most nights. Chaco is at an elevation of 6,200 feet (1,900 m), causing large temperature swings between night and day. Most years see fewer than 100 days free of frost.[1]

The few permanent streams near Chaco are mainly to the north. Some small springs provide water that seeps up from an underground aquifer. However, this water often has a high mineral content, making it poor for farming. Most surface water comes from arroyos, creeks that flow only when rain falls. Only approximately eight inches (20 cm) of rain falls in the basin annually.[2] It tends to

YOUNG ARCHAEOLOGIST

Gwinn Vivian had been involved in archaeology since he was a child. In an interview, he described how his interest arose at age 11. After World War II (1939–1945), his family moved to the canyon. Right away, he began searching for artifacts: "I spent the whole morning digging in the Pueblo Bonito refuse mound. I found a lot of potsherds, which I presented to my father at lunch."[3]

Sudden flooding still strikes the areas around Chaco Canyon today.

DANGER
DO NOT CROSS
IF WASH IS FLOWING

come in massive thunderstorms. The rain does not last long, but it leaves behind water flowing through arroyos such as Chaco Wash. These conditions are far from ideal for farming. Researchers worked to understand how the people of Chaco settled there and even thrived for centuries.

FARMING THE DESERT

The Ancestral Pueblo people worked hard to overcome their challenging climate. To make up for the erratic rainfall, the people of Chaco learned methods to control the water they received. These included a complex irrigation system.

The people of Chaco used dams and canals to direct water into fields. Masonry dams held floodwaters in reservoirs. Gates could control the flow, holding water until it was needed. One dam Vivian excavated was 120 feet (36 m) long, 20 feet (6 m) thick, and at least 7 feet (2 m) high. The earth and stone dam directed water through a 3.5-foot- (1 m) wide gate near the center. From the dam, water flowed into canals distributing water in a grid pattern through crop fields. The stone-lined canals were approximately 9 feet (3 m) wide and 2 to 5 feet (0.5–1.5 m) deep.[4] Mounds of earth bordered gardens of corn, beans, and squash, keeping water where it was most useful. This system worked well as long as each year provided enough rainfall.

As these water control projects got larger and more complex, they required more organization and labor. This may have contributed to social changes in Chaco society. Family groups had made most decisions in the past, but now different forms of leadership

WATER CONTROL

Water conservation involves farming areas that naturally receive water from rainfall or runoff. An example would be choosing to farm on floodplains that get rainfall drainage from other areas. Water diversion or irrigation captures and moves water using dams, canal systems, or other methods. This is a more complex and advanced practice than simple conservation.

might have developed. Smaller groups may have taken power. These new elite could have directed public projects and reinforced their social status through large construction projects and elaborate rituals. This shift may explain the great houses, large kivas, and exotic artifacts they left behind.

Irrigation allowed farmers to grow more crops. This may have helped the Chaco community develop. However, eventually the canyon soils became salty and depleted of nutrients. This made it increasingly difficult for farmers to produce enough food.

ROADS TO NOWHERE

While Gwinn Vivian was investigating irrigation systems in the early 1970s, he stumbled across some ancient roadways. During one excavation, he and a colleague realized the canal they were excavating was actually a road. This led to further study of the road system.

As early as 1901, surveyors had noted roads extending from the canyon. Aerial photographs

ANCIENT CEREMONIES

Anthropologist Brian Fagan imagined an ancient Pueblo ceremony:

The masked dancers move backward and forward in serried lines, the men in one row, the women in another. They sing in rhythm, facing one another, keeping the pace with their feet, progressing along the sides of the plaza. Brightly colored headdresses and masks adorn the dancers, who follow ancient routines, passed from generation to generation.[5]

Modern-day Pueblo people continue to hold ceremonies. Anthropologists can study them to make guesses at what the ancient ceremonies may have been like.

GWINN VIVIAN

At age one, R. Gwinnet Vivian arrived at Chaco Canyon when his father worked for the National Park Service. Vivian spent his life studying Southwestern archaeology. He was an early leader in cultural resource management. He worked with Native American communities and government officials to develop rules for historic preservation. At Chaco Canyon, his fieldwork focused on roads and water control systems. After retiring in 1999, Vivian became a lecturer and tour guide in the Chaco Canyon region.

Vivian's work helped inspire later preservation and study of the Chaco sites.

showed how extensive these roads were. Ground surveys demonstrated the astonishing amount of work that went into them.

Major roads were typically approximately 26 to 39 feet (8 to 12 m) across. Smaller roads averaged approximately 15 feet (4.5 m) across.[6] In some areas they crossed bare rock. In others, the roads were dug down below the ground's surface. The roads were edged with stones, masonry walls, low earthen mounds, or grooves. Instead of going around barriers such as mesas, the engineers built ramps. They even cut stairways into rock in Chaco Canyon's cliffs.

The Ancestral Pueblo people did not have vehicles or even beasts of burden. Some wondered why they would bother with such wide, highly engineered roads. In some places, four parallel roads were built within 60 yards (55 m) of each other.[7] Equally curious, some roads seemed to end in the middle of nowhere.

Archaeologists must sometimes fight assumptions based on their own cultural experiences. To modern people, roads are a way to move people or goods from one location to another. The archaeologists initially studying the Chaco road system developed theories based on this assumption. Some suggested the roads allowed laborers to carry the heavy roof beams used in the great houses. A few people thought armies marched on the roads.

However, the roads were most likely not simple links between communities. Most seem directed toward landmarks rather than other villages. In addition, archaeologists have found few signs of campsites or hearths alongside the roads. One would expect to find these things if travelers stayed overnight during longer journeys.

Besides, even armies or laborers carrying logs would not have needed such wide roads. Most likely, these travelers used ancient footpaths that followed the easiest route. Archaeologists continue debating the function of the Chaco road system, but many now believe the roads were primarily ceremonial.

BEYOND THE CANYON

The study of roads led to a greater awareness of other settlements connected to Chaco. Settlements known as outliers rose up throughout the region. Some were as far as 120 miles (193 km) from Chaco.[8] Most had a great house and a great kiva surrounded by small house sites. Some outliers had kivas four stories high. These might have been used to communicate at a

Stairways cut into the rock made it possible for the native people to enter and exit the canyon quickly.

distance with other towers in their line of sight along the roads, though this idea has been called into doubt by some archaeologists.

THE SALMON OUTLIER

Today, the Salmon Ruins are operated as a museum, library, and research center. Visitors can tour the ruins, including a great house, and visit a replica of a pit house. Archaeologists also continue working at the ruins. Several other outlier sites are open to visitors, including four within the Chaco Culture National Historical Park.

The Chaco Project research of the 1970s led to the idea of a "Chaco System." Supporters of this concept suggested Chaco was the center of a vast cultural network. Researchers believed these outlying communities were connected to Chaco because of many similarities. They all had great houses with similar construction methods, great kivas, and the same styles of pottery. While variations may exist between communities, the large number of similarities suggests a cultural connection.

Construction at some of these outlier sites sped up beginning around 1080. As drought caused a slowdown of activity at Chaco, other sites became more important. Two of the biggest and best known are Aztec and Salmon. Aztec lies approximately 50 miles (80 km) north of Chaco.[9] The site is thought to have taken over from Chaco as a major ritual center during the late 1100s. The Salmon outlier is approximately 45 miles (72 km) north of Chaco.[10] It was active from approximately 1088 to the late 1200s.

The Salmon Ruins were excavated in the 1970s.

There are more than 150 other outlier communities. Eventually, all of these were abandoned. During its heyday, however, Chaco influenced a vast area. Research conducted during the 1970s and 1980s, especially the Chaco Project, showed just how far Chaco culture had spread.

Looking to the Sky, Listening to the Past

The Chaco Project greatly increased archaeological knowledge about the canyon. Still, many mysteries remained. Some discoveries led to more questions. One research team surveyed the rock art around the canyon. They found many petroglyphs scraped into canyon walls and boulders. Designs included spirals and mazes along with animals, hands, and human figures. Some of these may have been clan symbols, identifying a particular group of people. Others recorded important events or might have been aids

Petroglyphs on the walls of Chaco Canyon's structures provide valuable insight into the culture of the buildings' residents.

SEASONS AND SOLSTICE

The sun rises in the east, but it does not rise in exactly the same spot each day. Rather, in the summer, the sun rises slightly to the northeast. It reaches its farthest northern point on approximately June 21. This date is the longest day of the year in the northern hemisphere and is known as the summer solstice. In the winter, the sun rises slightly south of true east. The shortest day of the year in the northern hemisphere is when the sun rises the farthest to the south. This is the winter solstice, approximately December 21. Many ancient cultures recognized these facts and built structures that would track the time of year based on the angle of the sun.

for remembering songs, stories, or ceremonies.

In 1977, artist Anna Sofaer spent the summer at Chaco as a volunteer recording rock art. On the second day of her visit, she and another volunteer climbed a steep hill, Fajada Butte, to record rock art there. Late in the day, they noticed a carved spiral in the shadow of three leaning rock slabs. They returned the next day to photograph it. In an interview, Sofaer remembered her revelation about the rock formation's significance:

We happened to get there near noon, a week from solstice, and a dagger of light was bisecting the spiral. It was formed by one of the openings of the three rock slabs in front of the spiral. I felt certain it was marking the summer solstice because the sharply pointed light shaft centered on the spiral created such a strong image.[1]

That image is now known as the Sun Dagger. At the summer solstice, a shaft of light pierces the center of the main spiral. During the winter solstice, two daggers of light bracket the spiral. At the spring and fall equinoxes, light shafts strike the center of a smaller spiral.

Sofaer began studying the architecture and rock art of Chaco as it relates to astronomy. She worked with colleagues who had backgrounds in astronomy and archaeology. Researchers found a large number of sites that seem to be ancient observatories. Some are simple, consisting of only a few circles carved on a rock face. Shafts of sunlight align with the marks at certain times of the year. These patterns may have been used

WRITING ON ROCK

Many cultures paint, pick, or scrape images into rock. A painted picture is called a pictograph. A picture picked or scraped into the rock surface is called a petroglyph. Scraping or chipping a design works best on cliff walls with a dark surface of natural varnish and lighter rock underneath. Pictographs used natural paints, often made from minerals. Petroglyphs and pictographs are not used as a written language. This distinguishes them from hieroglyphics, such as the symbols famously used by the ancient Egyptians.

The star and moon shapes in the petroglyphs at Chaco Canyon suggest the site's ancient residents were observers of the night sky.

to chart and celebrate the seasonal shifts of the sun or other celestial patterns. Keeping track of these patterns helped the ancient people decide when to plant crops, hold ceremonies and rituals, and do other seasonal activities.

More complex rock art was found near a great house called Peñasco Blanco. Three images are on the underside of a rock shelf in the cliff: a large star, a crescent moon, and a handprint. This might be a record of a supernova, the explosion of a large star, whose light reached Earth around July 4, 1054. At that time, a very bright star appeared in the sky and was visible during daytime for 23 days. At night, the supernova cast a ghostly red light. Some people believe the Chaco rock art images represent the supernova and the moon at the time when the supernova first appeared. The life-size hand shows the site is sacred.

On another panel below those images are three concentric circles with flames trailing to the right. This could be a record of Halley's Comet, which was visible in 1066. Another intriguing petroglyph can be found at a large boulder known as Piedra del Sol. Some people believe the boulder's rough circle with wavy tendrils represents a total solar eclipse.

Once people started looking for solar alignments, they found many possibilities at Chaco. For example, Pueblo Bonito is bisected by a wall that aligns with true north. There is also an unusual doorway set at a diagonal in the corner of a room. The doorway may have been used to track the sun. However, it is impossible to know what changes have happened to the site in recent centuries. Some of these supposed sky-watching stations might have been blocked by walls in ancient times.

ANCIENT ASTRONOMY

The Ancestral Pueblo people were not the only ancients to record astronomical events. Chinese astronomers described what they called guest stars, which were novae and supernovas. They recorded at least 75 of these between 532 BCE and 1064 CE. Both the Chinese and Japanese recorded the 1054 supernova. Arab and European astronomers also left records of celestial events. However, they do not seem to have made special note of the 1054 supernova.

No one has proven with certainty whether the Ancestral Pueblo intentionally used rock art as solar markers. Yet for some people, there are too many potential examples for it to be purely coincidence. Many scholars agree Chaco and outlier settlements show strong evidence of astronomy.

LEARNING FROM THE PRESENT

Although customs may have changed over the centuries, historic and modern practices provide clues to the past. Insight can come from the descendants of those who lived at the site in question. Anna Sofaer provided one example: "We shared our findings with several Pueblo people. Paul Pino, a war chief of Laguna Pueblo, spoke of the great spiritual significance that roads and the direction north hold for his people."[2] This information supports the idea of ceremonial roads and buildings being intentionally aligned to certain directions.

While Chaco Canyon was abandoned in approximately 1250, Hopi and Pueblo people continued making pilgrimages to Chaco. Richard Wetherill II described celebrations at Chaco Canyon from his childhood before 1910. "The Indians came from all around. The length of celebration would depend

Chaco's dark, clear skies make it an attractive location for astronomy even today.

WHERE ARE THEY NOW?

Public imagination seems to be captured by the idea of abandoned ruins and vanished people. Archaeologists can also sometimes fall into the trap of discussing the collapse of a society. However, in reality, few if any societies have ever truly collapsed. Rather, people move and cultural practices change. Today more than 60,000 Pueblo people live in the Southwest, mainly in northwestern New Mexico and northeastern Arizona.[4] According to one descendant, "They didn't abandon this place. It is still occupied. We can still pray to the spirits living in these places from as far away as our pueblo."[5]

on what kind they were having. Some would last one day, others lasted several days. . . . They had games, would throw rocks or sticks at a mark or something like that, and they had these rabbit hunts."[3] It is possible similar rituals took place at Chaco a millennium ago.

Archaeologists and anthropologists talk to present-day indigenous people to gain a better understanding of the past. In the 1940s, an archaeologist uncovered a rich burial site near Flagstaff, Arizona. He took some of the grave goods to Hopi elders. Several elders independently agreed the artifacts pertained to a witchcraft ceremony. The ceremony was no longer performed, but the elders could describe elements of it. They also correctly predicted other artifacts the archaeologists would find in the grave. Modern Pueblo societies share many traditions with their ancestors, including elements of agriculture, architecture, and ritual. Songs and stories give insight into ancient society.

There are many challenges to interpreting the past through the Pueblo people of today, however. The

Spanish entered the Southwest in the 1500s and brutally conquered most Pueblos. Some cultural practices ended, while many continued in secret to avoid conflict. Later, European colonization and the modern industrial society caused additional pressure. Some practices have changed over time and in response to outside pressure. Today's Pueblo people are often secretive about some customs and rituals. They may refuse to share details with archaeologists and other outsiders.

Cultural anthropologists have also looked at historic and modern Pueblo societies for clues to the political structure at Chaco. In historic Pueblo societies, no single person or family ruled. Rather, political power came from a complex network of ritual organizations. Many researchers have suggested leadership at Chaco may have been similar. However, there is no way of proving it. Still, the more evidence researchers collect, the more accurate their theories are likely to be.

8

Ongoing Questions

We may never have answers to all the questions about Chaco Canyon. Even the most accepted theories can be challenged as new evidence or new interpretations arise. For example, many people believed drought drove the Ancestral Pueblo people out of the canyon. This theory was backed by evidence from tree-ring dating which indicated a long dry spell around the time people left the canyon.

Exactly why the people of Chaco Canyon abandoned their grand settlements remains a mystery.

But in the 1990s, new climate studies suggested the drought was not bad enough to force people to abandon their settlement. In addition, the people of Chaco began leaving before the drought. Perhaps drought was part of the problem, but not the whole story.

New theories arose. Wars or religious crises may have combined with climate challenges to cause the movement. Changes in rainfall patterns and temperature could have created additional pressures on farming. Several factors may have combined. Drought and low rainfall could have caused people to lose faith in their religious leaders. That might have led to political and cultural changes, encouraging migration. Different archaeologists have their own preferred theories, but we will likely never know the truth for certain.

One of the biggest challenges in understanding Chaco is that it was not frozen at a single moment in time. Chaco was slowly abandoned over decades. Archaeologist David Wilcox has said, "We see these places, and we think of them as static, as doorways and walls that are solid. But they weren't. They were spaces meant to serve purposes, and those purposes were fluid, changing by generations, or yearly, or even daily."[1]

LOOKING FORWARD

Researchers have plenty of work ahead. The University of New Mexico runs a program of field investigations in Chaco Canyon. The hope is to contribute to a greater understanding of the elements at work during the height of Chaco culture between 850 and 1140. Researchers from different fields are studying farming, technology, and socioeconomic changes.

Outlier sites are also the subject of investigations. Chimney Rock is an outlier community in southwestern Colorado. It appears to have been in use for only approximately 50 years. Excavation occurred in the early 1970s,

Archaeologists believe it is important to remember the living spaces of Chaco Canyon were once bustling with daily activity.

and in the late 1980s the site became known for its astronomy connections. A University of Colorado at Boulder team began new excavations in 2009. It found pottery, stone tools, animal bones, burned ears of corn, and the remains of ancient timbers. These discoveries may provide new insights into the ancient people who lived there.

New finds can also expand on past research. Chimney Rock was dated through tree rings, but new wood samples might provide more detail about construction there. More data means a better understanding of the chronology. New information can also confirm or challenge previous ideas.

The science of studying tree rings has gotten more advanced since its development in the 1930s. Experts use equations to estimate the rainfall and temperature of a given year based on the size of the tree ring.

TODAY'S ARCHAEOLOGISTS

Archaeology changed dramatically in the 1900s. The standard archaeologist is no longer an amateur explorer searching for treasure. Today, the National Park Service defines the minimum education and experience employees must have. Archaeologists should have a graduate degree in archaeology, anthropology, or a closely related field. They must also have professional field experience. However, university students may have opportunities to study at sites such as Chaco before finishing their degrees.

This can suggest how well crops might have done in a particular region at a specific time.

Dendrochronology has also split into secondary studies. At the University of Arizona's Laboratory of Tree-Ring Research, scientists explore many uses for tree-ring data. Tree-ring analysis is used in climate and environmental studies and much more. This research can help archaeologists understand the landscape of the past.

Technological advances provide new tools in other areas as well. The team at Chimney Rock analyzed corn samples for their mineral content to identify where the corn was grown. Studies like this can show whether ancient people grew their own food or imported it from other regions.

New dating techniques such as radiocarbon dating allow experts to identify the age of tiny samples. DNA studies help researchers track the movements of people over centuries. As archaeology expanded as a science, many subspecialties sprang up. Archaeologists may specialize in the study of pottery, human bones, or ancient diets. They may work with other experts in

CHOCOLATE FROM THE PAST

From 2004 to 2007, a University of New Mexico team returned to trenches first dug in the 1920s. It recovered hundreds of thousands of potsherds. A ceramics specialist, Patricia Crown, chose samples for analysis. Three samples from cylinder jars showed traces of cacao, or chocolate. This likely came from central Mexico, where cacao was drunk in rituals.

VISITING CHACO CANYON

Today up to 50,000 people visit Chaco Canyon every year.[2] A visitor center includes a museum, bookstore, and theater. A nine-mile (14 km) loop road passes five major sites, including Pueblo Bonito. At each site, visitors can walk along short trails. Longer hiking trails lead to more remote sites, passing ancient roads and petroglyphs. Guided hikes, tours, and speakers are available for tourists who wish to learn more.

fields ranging from botany to insect studies to climate research. Archaeology happens both in the field and in the lab.

Despite the amount of information already collected, there is always more to be found. In 2009, a backhoe digging at a pumping station in Chaco Canyon unearthed a pot, which led archaeologists to discover a new site. The site was dated to approximately 500–600 CE, at the time of the Basketmakers.

The fact that new artifacts are waiting to be found is exciting for archaeologists, but the ease of finding some artifacts also causes problems. Tourists to Chaco Canyon have found many potsherds and other objects. It is illegal to remove these finds, but visitors sometimes take them home as souvenirs. Some people later feel guilty and mail back the artifacts. These items can then be used for exhibits or other educational projects. However, without detailed information about where they were found, some of the knowledge they could have provided is lost.

The fragile walls of Chaco Canyon's buildings are highly susceptible to weathering and damage.

CHACO IN DANGER

Maintaining a site like Chaco Canyon is not a cheap or simple process. Summer thunderstorms and winter snows damage ancient walls. Windstorms and extreme temperatures add to the threat. Vandalism and looting are a problem. Even law-abiding people can cause fragile ruins to deteriorate when they visit in large numbers.

As more archaeologists, government officials, and members of the public began taking an interest, the canyon gained protection. In 1980,

WHO'S IN CHARGE?

Many people have an interest in exploring Chaco Canyon. Others feel just as strongly about preserving it. Archaeologists, Native Americans, and tourists may have different priorities. The park's Cultural Resources Division is tasked with resolving these tensions. In the past, the archaeological community primarily guided park policy. In recent years, the park's American Indian Consultation Committee has taken a lead role. Ideally, people work together to find solutions that satisfy everyone.

the national monument was enlarged to include neighboring communities. It was renamed the Chaco Culture National Historical Park. The United Nations Educational, Scientific and Cultural Organization (UNESCO) named it a World Heritage Site in 1987 in recognition of its worldwide cultural importance. The park is one of only 20 UNESCO World Heritage sites in the United States. The World Heritage Committee recommended including other examples of Pueblo culture in the designation. Aztec Ruins, Salmon Ruins, and several other sites are part of the Heritage Site.

In 1996, the World Monuments Fund included Chaco on its list of 100 Most Endangered Monuments. It is also considered one of the ten most endangered national parks. The National Park Service is trying to update the management plan to address concerns. Volunteer organizations are providing funds and labor to maintain and protect the park.

Research continues, but the focus has shifted away from large excavations. Archaeologists are more aware of Native American concerns today. Many

Native people believe their ancestors should be left undisturbed. They do not approve of excavations that may uncover the bodies of their ancestors. Remote sensing allows archaeologists to gather data without disturbing sites.

Funding is always a concern, so resources must be used wisely. One effective use of resources involves concentrating on what has already been found. Researchers are reexamining museum collections and other artifacts from past days. With new technology and new ideas, these old finds may have more to reveal.

Making past research accessible is also a priority. Various people and organizations have excavated at Chaco for more than a century. The artifacts, photographs, drawings, and notes from these digs are scattered around the country. Researchers need access to the data in order to study Chaco properly. The Chaco Digital Initiative is attempting to create a

PROTECTING THE DARKNESS

Protecting the Chaco Canyon site involves more than buildings and artifacts. In September 2013, the International Dark Sky Association certified the Chaco Culture National Historical Park as an official International Dark Sky Park. This signifies that the lack of manmade light sources make the park an outstanding place to observe stars, planets, and other features of the night sky. Park authorities carefully control light pollution to make this possible. The park's strict outdoor lighting guidelines preserve the dark sky, making it a popular observation destination for people from all around the world.

comprehensive digital archive. This will make the information widely available to researchers and the public.

Previously excavated sites must also be preserved. Once a ruin is exposed to the elements, it can deteriorate quickly. To preserve these sites for future study—and for the enjoyment of the public—they must be properly protected.

From early explorers to today's tourists, Chaco has captured the imaginations of millions. More than a century of archaeology has greatly expanded our understanding of the Ancestral Pueblo people. Each decade sees new research and new technology to broaden and clarify the past, yet questions remain for future generations to explore. The mysteries of Chaco will continue intriguing archaeologists and visitors alike.

Preserving the structures of Chaco Canyon is a priority for the workers at the Chaco Culture National Historical Park.

TIMELINE

6500–1200 BCE
Hunter-gatherers live around Chaco Canyon.

1200 BCE–750 CE
People settle in homes during the Basketmaker periods.

1054
On July 4, the light of a supernova reaches Earth and is possibly recorded in Chaco rock art.

1140–1150
The Chaco System declines and people move out of the great houses.

1700s
Navajo families settle near Chaco Canyon.

1849
US Army surveyors explore Chaco Canyon with the help of Native American guides.

1896

Richard Wetherill and George Pepper begin excavating, primarily at Pueblo Bonito.

1907

On March 11, President Theodore Roosevelt creates the Chaco Canyon National Monument.

1970–1985

The Chaco Project conducts research at Chaco Canyon in many fields.

1977

On June 29, artist Anna Sofaer realizes a rock art image may mark the summer solstice.

1987

Chaco Canyon becomes a UNESCO World Heritage Site.

2013

Chaco Canyon is designated as an official International Dark Sky Park.

DIGGING UP THE FACTS

DATE OF DISCOVERY

Chaco Canyon was first recorded on a Spanish map in 1774 and noted by the governor of New Mexico in 1823. The US Army surveyed it in 1849. The first official excavations started in 1896.

KEY PLAYERS

- Richard Wetherill, a rancher and amateur archaeologist, was the first to establish an official dig at Chaco Canyon.

- Gordon Vivian excavated at Chaco as a student and then worked at the canyon as a Park Service archaeologist. He developed ruin stabilization techniques and started water and road surveys.

- Dr. John Corbett, chief archaeologist for the National Park Service, organized the Chaco Project to address questions about Chaco.

KEY TECHNOLOGIES

- Dendrochronology, a tree-ring dating system, was used to date the buildings at Chaco Canyon. Data found at Chaco helped extend the tree-ring timeline.

- Pottery research at Chaco Canyon led to a pottery classification system. Florence Hawley published a manual on southwestern ceramics in 1936.

- Remote-sensing technology showed a vast system of roads connecting Chaco Canyon to outlier settlements.

IMPACT ON SCIENCE

Archaeologists developed the concept of the Chaco System, the idea that Chaco was the center of a vast cultural network. Rock art studies led to the realization that the Ancestral Pueblo people may have made astronomy observations. The Chaco Digital Initiative is collecting and digitizing research records and making them available to the public.

EXPLORING CHACO CANYON

There are several ways to explore Chaco Canyon today. Beginning from the park's visitor center, a nine-mile (14 km) paved road circles the area and lets visitors access five major sites. Smaller trails branch off at each of the sites. The paved road can also be biked. Hardier travelers can hike dirt trails to several more remote sites.

QUOTE

"We see these places, and we think of them as static, as doorways and walls that are solid. But they weren't. They were spaces meant to serve purposes, and those purposes were fluid, changing by generations, or yearly, or even daily."—*David Wilcox*

GLOSSARY

absolute dating
The process of estimating the age of an item.

Anasazi
A Navajo word meaning "ancient ones" or "ancient enemy," previously used to refer to ancient people who lived in Chaco and other parts of the northern US Southwest.

aquifer
An underground layer of rock that is permeable, so it can hold water.

arroyo
A gully with steep sides cut by water.

atlatl
A device Native Americans used for hunting and in warfare for throwing a spear or dart.

masonry
Stonework.

mesa
A flat-topped hill with steep sides in a generally flat landscape.

nomenclature
A system of defining names in a particular field of study.

outlier
A community outside of Chaco Canyon that was probably linked to Chaco.

petroglyph
An image that has been carved into rock.

pictograph
An image painted onto a rock.

pothunter
Someone who digs archaeological sites without permission in order to sell artifacts or keep them in a personal collection.

potsherd
A broken piece of a ceramic vessel.

stratigraphy
The study of layers in the ground.

veneer
A thin decorative covering.

ADDITIONAL RESOURCES

SELECTED BIBLIOGRAPHY

Childs, Craig. *House of Rain: Tracking a Vanished Civilization Across the American Southwest*. New York: Little, Brown, 2007. Print.

Fagan, Brian. *Chaco Canyon: Archaeologists Explore the Lives of an Ancient Society*. Oxford, New York: Oxford UP, 2005. Print.

FURTHER READINGS

Fleck, John. *The Tree Rings' Tale: Understanding Our Changing Climate (Worlds of Wonder)*. Albuquerque, NM: U of New Mexico P, 2009. Print.

Lourie, Peter. *The Lost World of the Anasazi: Exploring the Mysteries of Chaco Canyon*. Honesdale, PA: Boyds Mills, 2007. Print.

WEBSITES

To learn more about Digging Up the Past, visit **booklinks.abdopublishing.com**. These links are routinely monitored and updated to provide the most current information available.

FOR MORE INFORMATION

For more information on this subject, contact or visit the following organizations:

CHACO CULTURE NATIONAL HISTORICAL PARK

PO Box 220

Nageezi, NM 87037

505-786-7014 ext. 221

http://www.nps.gov/chcu/index.htm

Chaco Canyon is located in northwestern New Mexico. Visitors can tour the ruins, listen to talks, and view the museum. The website provides information on the park, plus links to the research archive documenting the history of archaeological research in Chaco Canyon.

SALMON RUINS

6131 Highway 64

Bloomfield, NM 87413

505-632-2013

http://www.salmonruins.com

Visitors to the Salmon outlier community can tour ruins, a Chaco great house, and a homestead from the 1800s.

SOURCE NOTES

Chapter 1. Secrets of the Past

1. "Chaco Culture NHP and University of Virginia Collaborate on the Chaco Digital Initiative." *Archaeology Program*. National Park Service, 2013. Web. 20 June 2013.

2. Brian Fagan. *Chaco Canyon: Archaeologists Explore the Lives of an Ancient Society*. New York: Oxford UP, 2005. Print. 3.

3. "History & Culture." *Chaco Culture*. National Park Service, 2013. Web. 18 June 2013.

Chapter 2. Exploring the Southwest

1. Frank McNitt. *Richard Wetherill: Anasazi*. Albuquerque, NM: U of New Mexico P, 1966. Print. 107.

2. Ibid. 36.

3. "Chaco Culture NHP and University of Virginia Collaborate on the Chaco Digital Initiative." *Archaeology Program*. National Park Service, 2013. Web. 20 June 2013.

4. Frank McNitt. *Richard Wetherill: Anasazi*. Albuquerque, NM: U of New Mexico P, 1966. Print. 113.

5. Richard N. Sandlin. "Excerpts from an Interview with Richard Wetherill." *Wetherill Family*. Wetherill Family, Jan. 1978. Web. 8 June 2013.

6. "Chaco Culture NHP and University of Virginia Collaborate on the Chaco Digital Initiative." *Archaeology Program*. National Park Service, 2013. Web. 20 June 2013.

7. Richard N. Sandlin. "Excerpts from an Interview with Richard Wetherill." *Wetherill Family*. Wetherill Family, Jan. 1978. Web. 8 June 2013.

8. Frank McNitt. *Richard Wetherill: Anasazi*. Albuquerque, NM: U of New Mexico P, 1966. Print. 113.

Chapter 3. Searching for Clues

1. Neil Judd. "Smithsonian Miscellaneous Collections Volume 124: The Material Culture of Pueblo Bonito." *Smithsonian*. Smithsonian, 29 Dec. 1954. Web. 21 June 2013.

2. Ibid.

3. Ibid.

4. Ibid.

5. Stephen H. Lekson. "Ancient Chaco's New History." *Archaeology Southwest*. Center for Desert Archaeology, Winter 2000. Web. 20 June 2013.

6. "The Great Houses." *Exploratorium*. Exploratorium, n.d. Web. 20 June 2013.

7. Bijal P. Trivedi. "Ancient Timbers Reveal Secrets of Anasazi Builders." *National Geographic Today*. National Geographic, 28 Sept. 2001. Web. 20 June 2013.

Chapter 4. Beyond Pueblo Bonito

1. Lynne D. Escue. "Chaco Culture National Historic Park." *First People*. First People, n.d. Web. 4 July 2013.

2. Richard N. Sandlin. "Excerpts from an Interview with Richard Wetherill." *Wetherill Family*. Wetherill Family, Jan. 1978. Web. 8 June 2013.

Chapter 5. The Chaco Project

1. "Archaeological Collection." *Chaco Culture*. National Park Service, 2013. Web. 22 June 2013.

2. Ibid.

3. Maru Maruca. "An Administrative History of the Chaco Project." *National Park Service*. National Park Service, 1982. Web. 31 Dec. 2013.

4. "Archaeological Collection." *Chaco Culture*. National Park Service, 2013. Web. 22 June 2013.

5. R. Gwinn Vivian and Bruce Hilpert. *The Chaco Handbook*. Salt Lake City, UT: U of Utah P, 2002. Print 217–218.

6. Craig Childs. *House of Rain: Tracking a Vanished Civilization across the American Southwest*. New York: Little, 2007. Print. 47–48.

7. Ibid. 48.

8. Brian Fagan. *Chaco Canyon: Archaeologists Explore the Lives of an Ancient Society*. New York: Oxford UP, 2005. Print. 140.

9. Ibid. 165.

Chapter 6. Water and Roads

1. "Weather." *Chaco Culture*. National Park Service, 2013. Web. 22 June 2013.

2. Ibid.

3. R. Gwinn Vivian and Margaret Anderson. *Chaco Canyon*. New York: Oxford UP, 2002. Print. 42.

4. Kendrick Frazier. *People of Chaco: A Canyon and Its Culture*. New York: Norton, 2005. Print. 100–102.

5. Brian Fagan. *Chaco Canyon: Archaeologists Explore the Lives of an Ancient Society*. New York: Oxford UP, 2005. Print. 181.

6. Ibid. 167.

7. Ibid. 21.

8. Ibid. 20–21.

9. Ibid. 205.

10. Ibid. 208.

Chapter 7. Looking to the Sky, Listening to the Past

1. Robert Wilder. "Anna Sofaer." *El Palacio*. Solstice Project, 2013. Web. 27 June 2013.

2. Ibid.

3. Richard N. Sandlin. "Excerpts from an Interview with Richard Wetherill." *Wetherill Family*. Wetherill Family, Jan. 1978. Web. 8 June 2013.

4. "Pueblo People Today." *Crow Canyon Archaeological Center*. Crow Canyon Archaeological Center, 2011. Web. 27 June 2013.

5. Mark Varien and Richard H. Wilshusen. *Seeking The Center Place*. Salt Lake City: U of Utah P, 2002. Print. 260.

Chapter 8. Ongoing Questions

1. Craig Childs. *House of Rain: Tracking a Vanished Civilization across the American Southwest*. New York: Little, 2007. Print. 26.

2. Jane Schneider. "New Visitor Center and Museum at Chaco Culture National Historical Park Come With Challenges." *National Parks Traveler*. National Parks Traveler, 21 Sept. 2010. Web. 28 June 2013.

INDEX

ABOUT THE AUTHOR

Chris Eboch writes fiction and nonfiction for all ages. Her recent nonfiction titles include *Living with Dyslexia*, *The Green Movement*, and *Magnets in the Real World*. Her novels for young people include historical fiction, ghost stories, and action-packed adventures.

ABOUT THE CONSULTANT

Jakob Sedig is a PhD candidate at the University of Colorado, Boulder. Jakob has worked at numerous archaeological sites across the US Southwest, including Homol'ovi Ruins, the Crow Canyon Archaeological Center, Chimney Rock, Casas Grandes, Black Mountain, and Woodrow Ruin. His previous research in the Southwest focused on stone tools, particularly the ceremonial and symbolic use of projectile points in the northern San Juan region. Jakob currently works in the Mimbres region of southwest New Mexico. His dissertation research has focused on Woodrow Ruin, and the social, demographic, and environmental changes that occurred there and in the Mimbres region between 900 and 1000 CE.